CONFIDENT | The Biblical Account of How Daniel Overcame the Lions' Den

© 2019 Adalis Shuttlesworth

All rights reserved. This book or parts thereof may not be reproduced in any form, stored in any retrieval system, or transmitted in any form by any means—electronic, mechanical, photocopy, recording, or otherwise—without prior written permission of the publisher, except as provided by United States of America copyright law. For permission requests, write to the publisher, at "Attention: Permissions Coordinator," at the address below.

ISBN - 978-0-9981753-4-8

Revival Today
PO Box 254
Oakdale, PA, 15071
RevivalToday.com

Illustrated by Justin Stewart
Justifii.com

For information about special discounts available for bulk purchases, sales promotions, fund-raising and educational needs, contact Revival Today Sales at 412-787-2578 or info@revivaltoday.com

DISCLAIMER:
This is *NOT* the Bible. Read your Bible!

CONFIDENT

The Biblical Account Of How Daniel Overcame the Lions Den

by

ADALIS SHUTTLESWORTH

illustrated by

JUSTIN STEWART

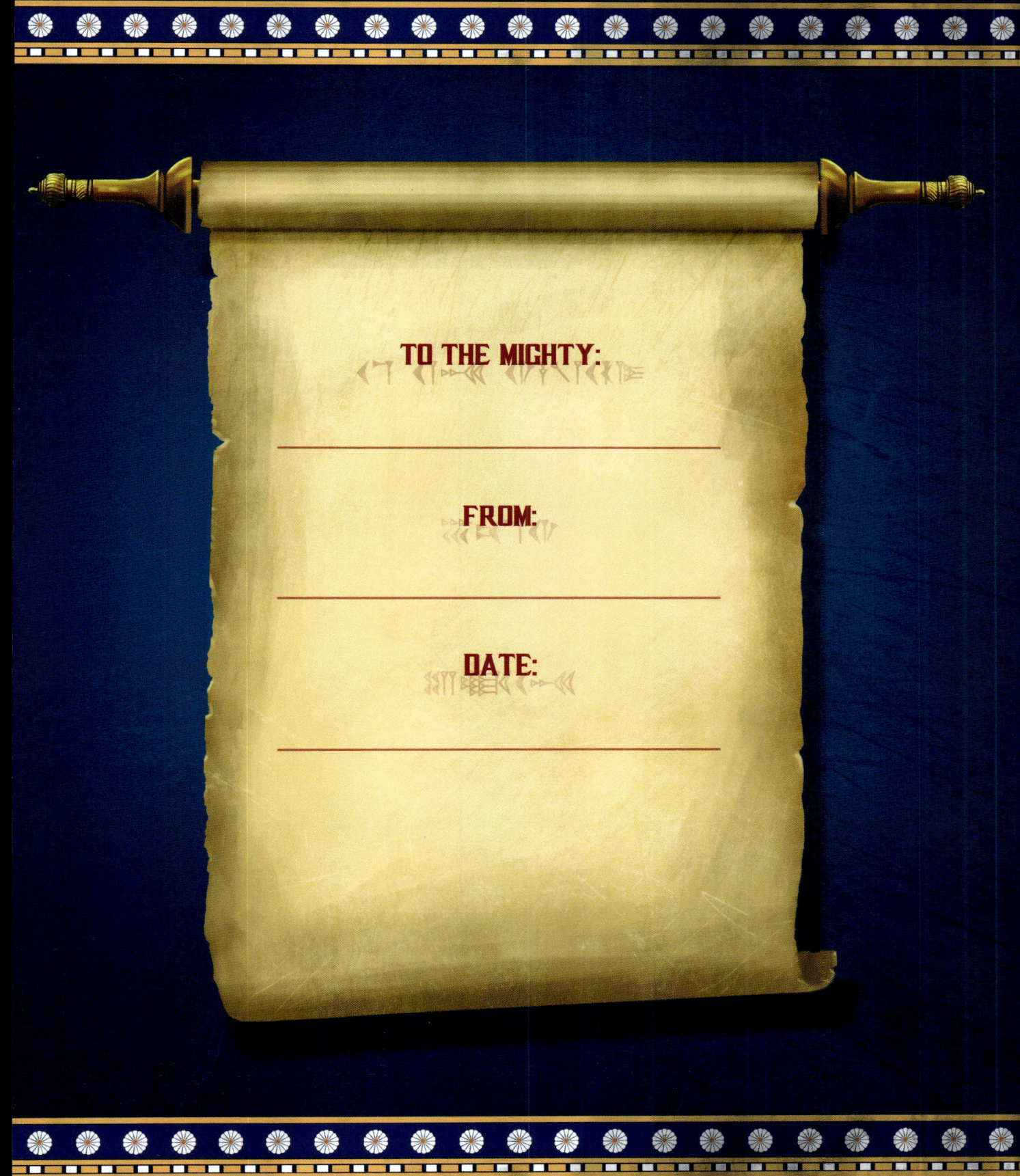

ABOUT THE MIGHTY SERIES

The Mighty Series is a compilation of children's books taken directly from the Word of God without the side of political correctness. There isn't a junior Holy Spirit for kids; they can walk in the fullness of their calling and destiny right now. The Bible says in Joel 2:28, "Your sons and daughters will prophecy..." The Bible is filled with promises for our children! As you read these books to them, know that you are ministering to their spirits, and building them up to be everything God has called them to be!

A LETTER TO PARENTS

I am beyond excited to share this series with you! As a mother, I fully understand the need for a more precise understanding of biblical principles. Our children do not need a watered down version of The Bible - they are brilliant, unaffected by doubt, and not jaded. During Childhood is the best time to begin to instill Godly principles in the life of your child that will have lifelong impact. They will learn, through the life of Daniel, how to have unshakeable confidence in God while staring the enemy in the face!

ADALIS SHUTTLESWORTH
FOUNDER & AUTHOR OF THE MIGHTY SERIES

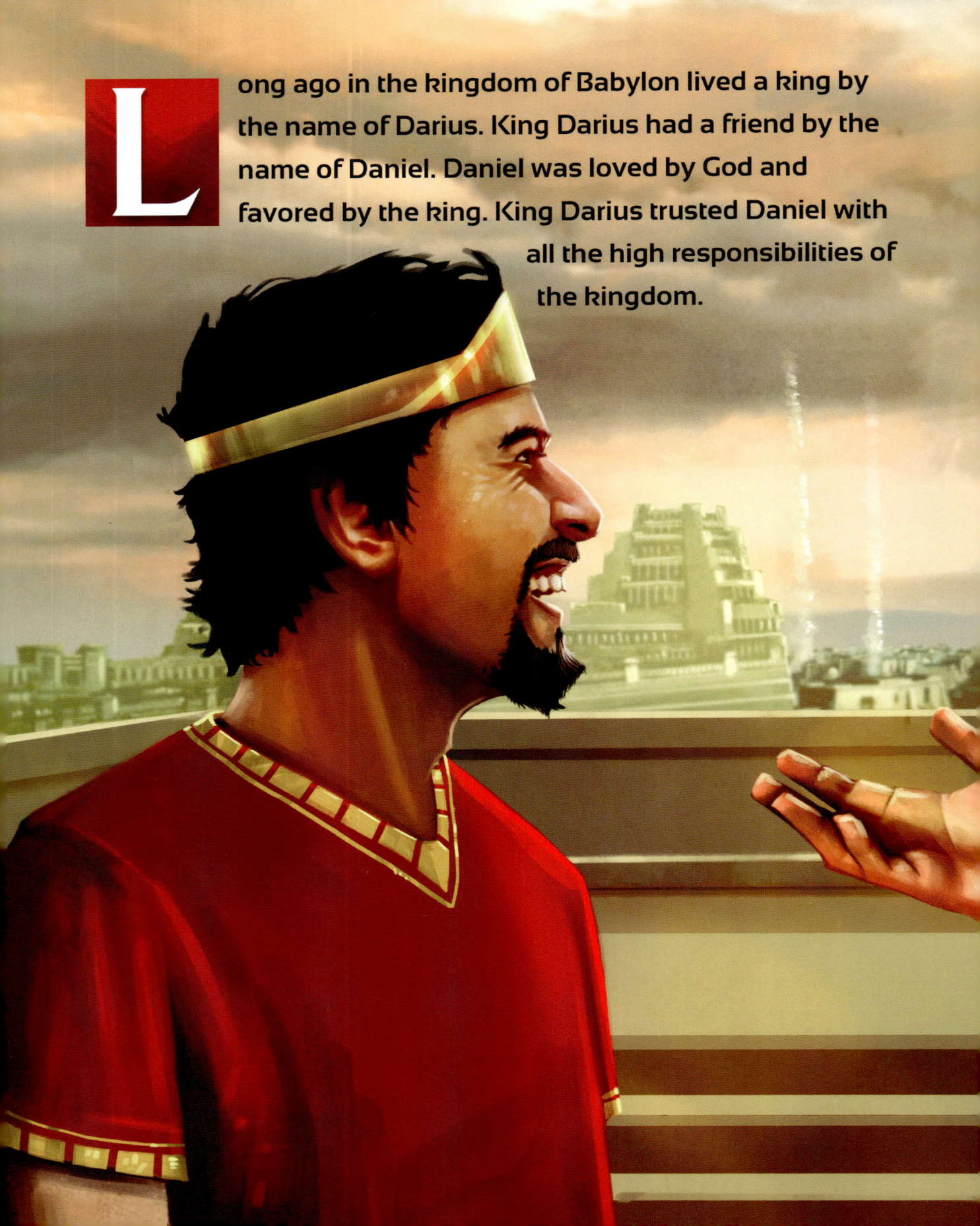

Long ago in the kingdom of Babylon lived a king by the name of Darius. King Darius had a friend by the name of Daniel. Daniel was loved by God and favored by the king. King Darius trusted Daniel with all the high responsibilities of the kingdom.

The other kingdom officials were jealous of Daniel and his favor with the king. They gathered together to plot against Daniel. They searched and searched but could find no fault in Daniel. He was faithful to the king, very responsible, and trustworthy.

"OUR ONLY CHANCE TO DESTROY DANIEL IS TO ATTACK HIS RELIGION!"

They concluded.

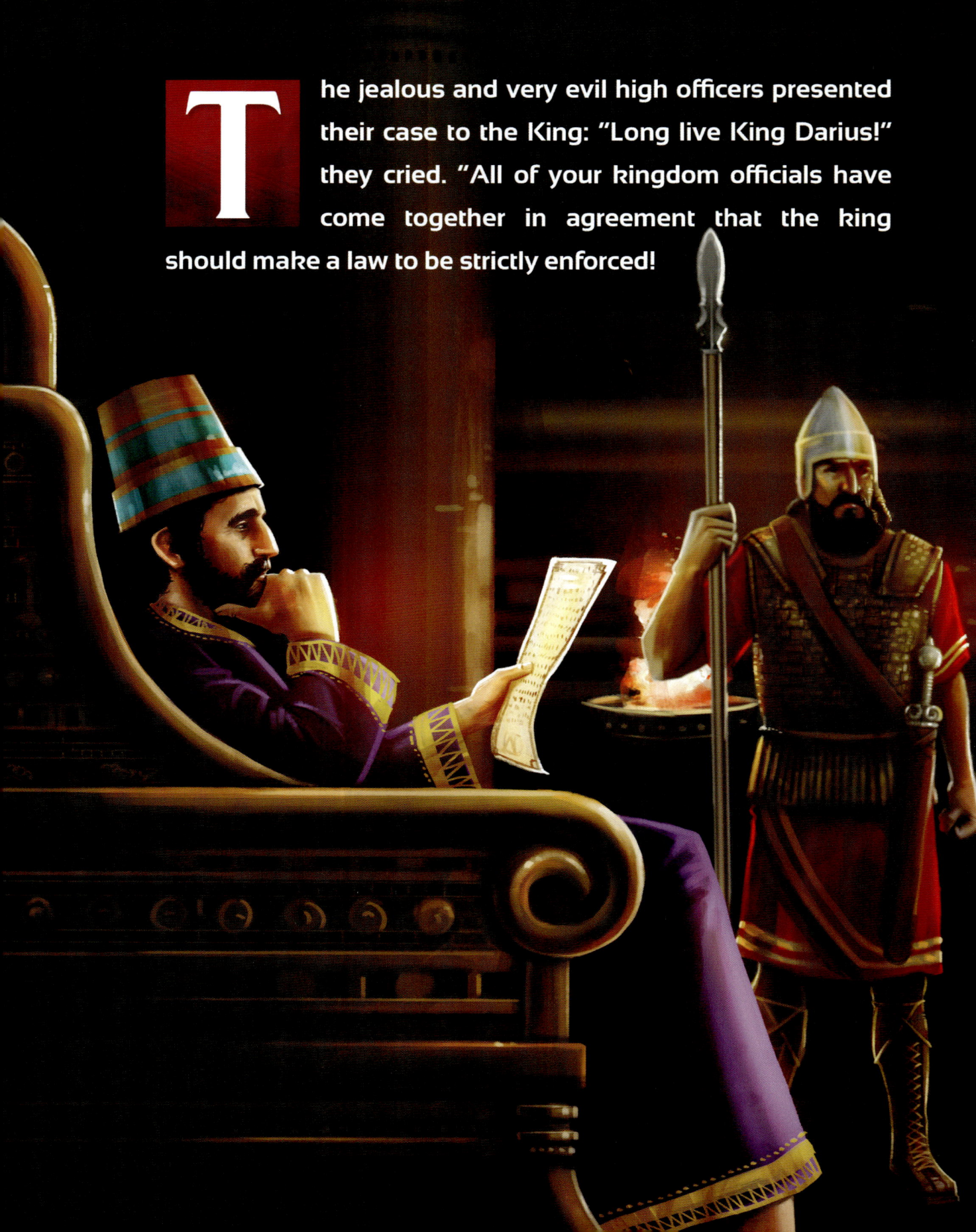

The jealous and very evil high officers presented their case to the King: "Long live King Darius!" they cried. "All of your kingdom officials have come together in agreement that the king should make a law to be strictly enforced!

Establish a new decree that anyone who prays to any God or human, other than you, be put in the den of lions. Now Your Majesty, sign this law that cannot be canceled or changed."

SO, KING DARIUS SIGNED THE AGREEMENT.

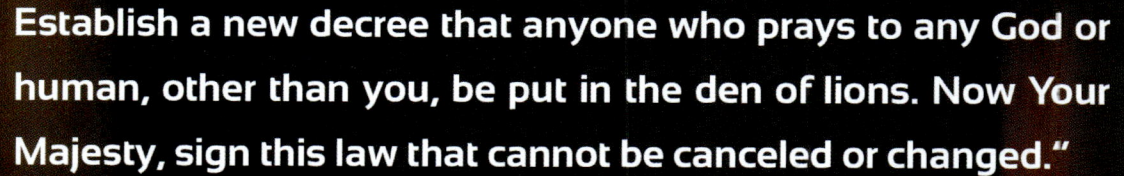

When Daniel found out the law had been signed he went home to pray, as he usually did. He knelt down as usual in his room upstairs with the windows opened towards God's Holy City, Jerusalem. Daniel prayed three times a day and gave thanks to God.

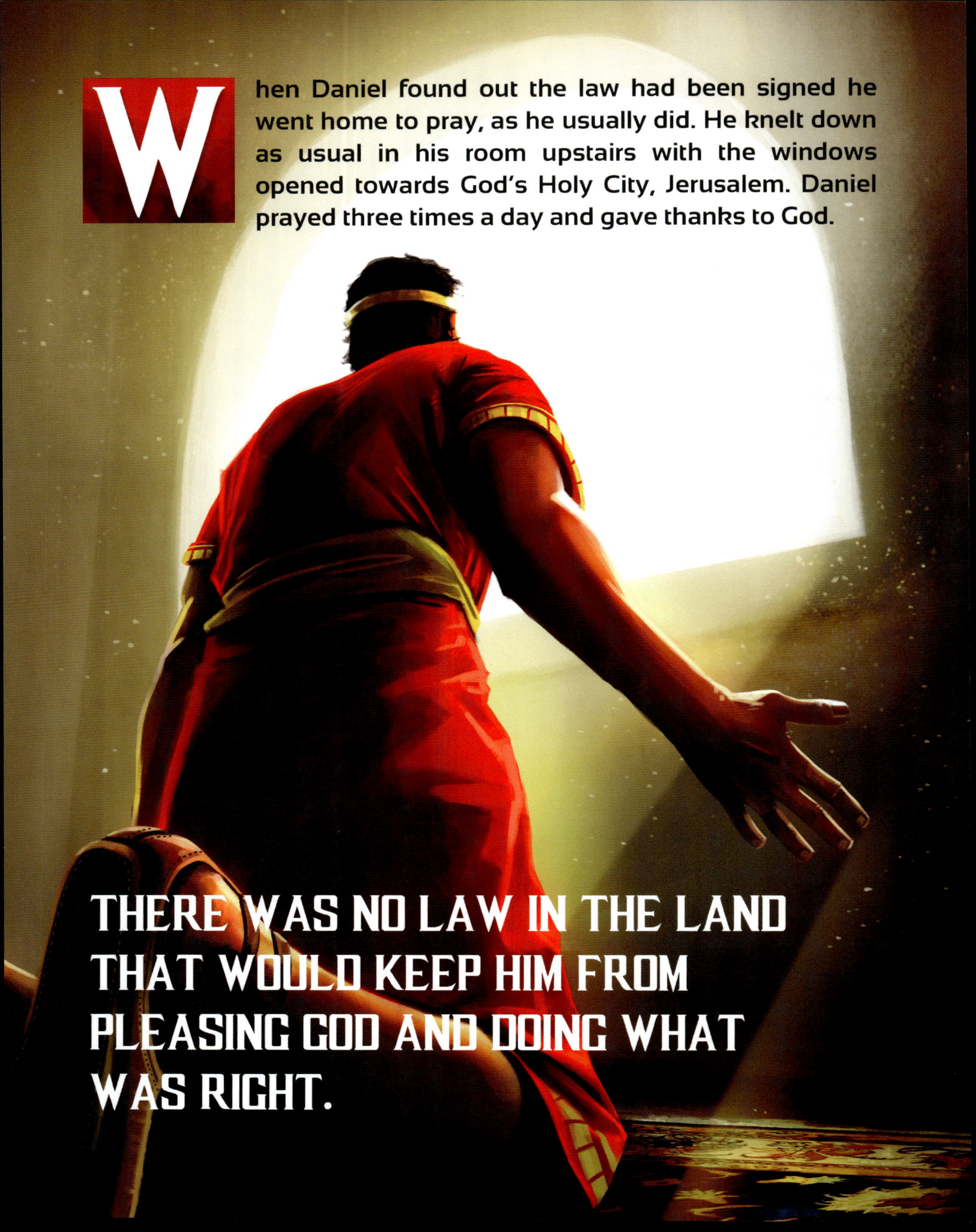

THERE WAS NO LAW IN THE LAND THAT WOULD KEEP HIM FROM PLEASING GOD AND DOING WHAT WAS RIGHT.

These evil officers knew Daniel would be praying, so they went to check up on him.

THEY FOUND DANIEL KNEELING, ASKING GOD FOR HELP.

The men went back to the king and reported what had happened. "Did you not make a decree, Your Majesty, that anyone who prays to any god or human other than you would be thrown into the lions' den?"

King Darius answered, "The decree stands according to the law of this kingdom."

"**THIS MAN DANIEL, PAYS NO ATTENTION TO YOU OR THE DECREE YOU'VE PUT IN WRITING.**

HE STILL PRAYS TO HIS GOD THREE TIMES A DAY"

They explained.

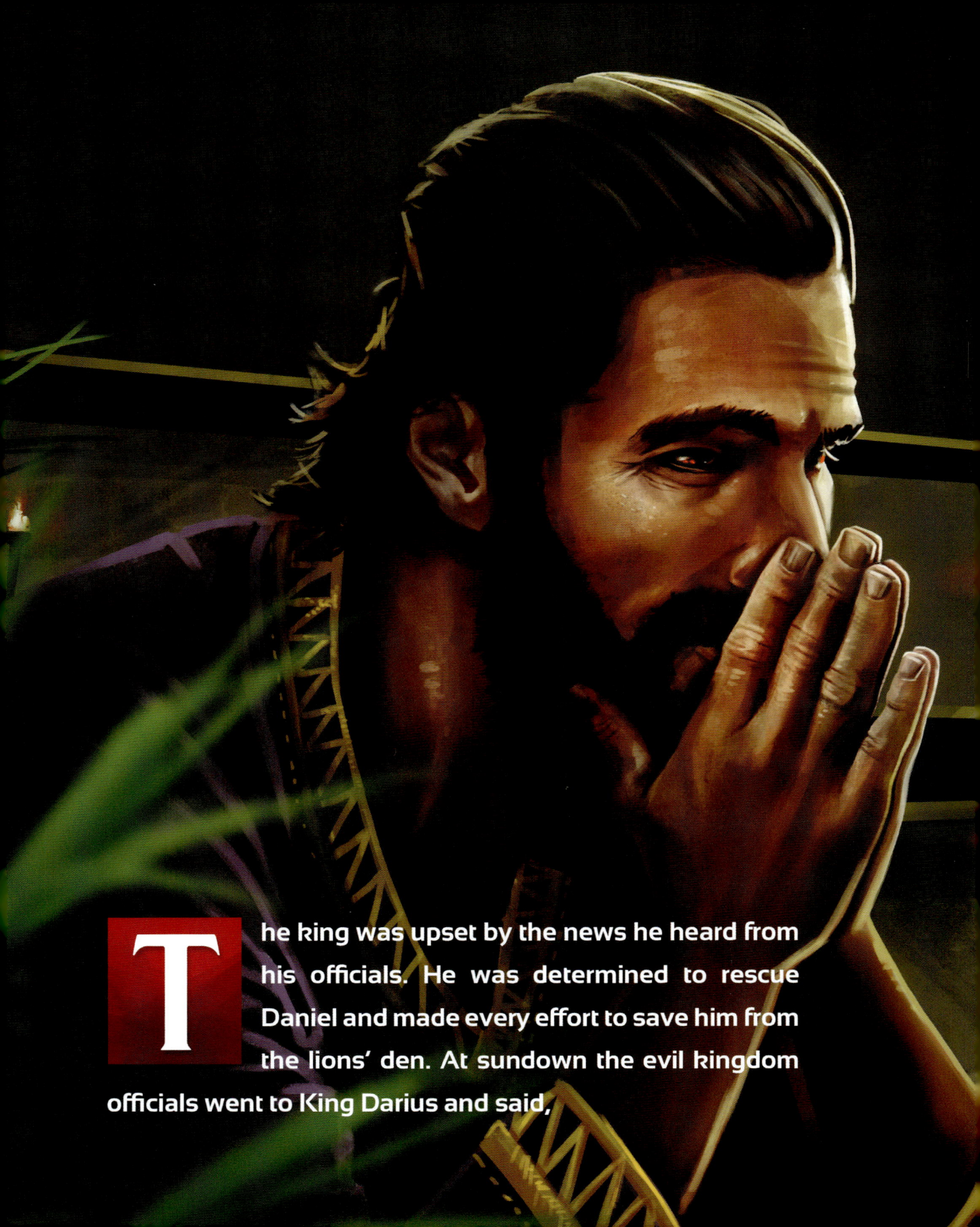

The king was upset by the news he heard from his officials. He was determined to rescue Daniel and made every effort to save him from the lions' den. At sundown the evil kingdom officials went to King Darius and said,

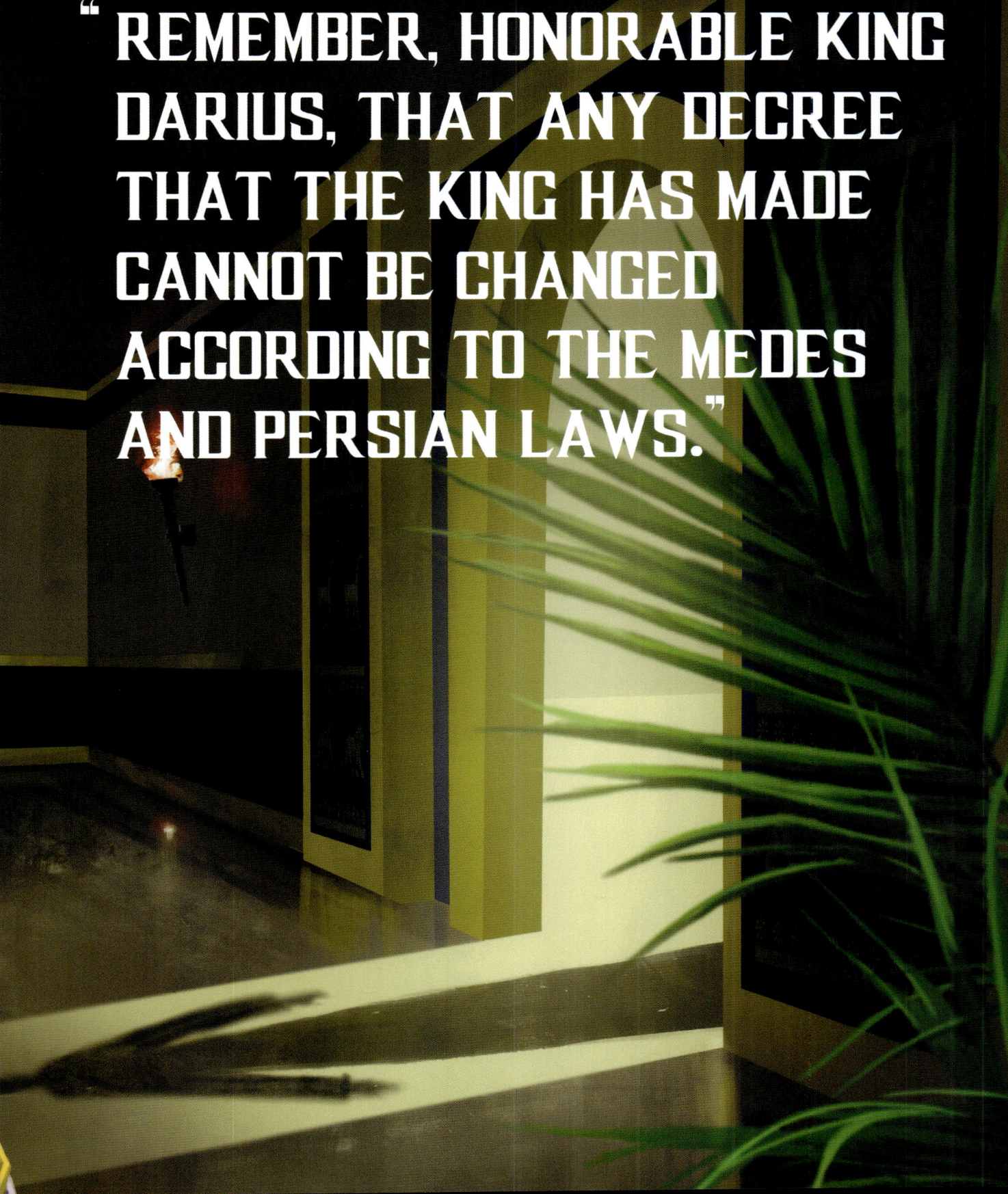

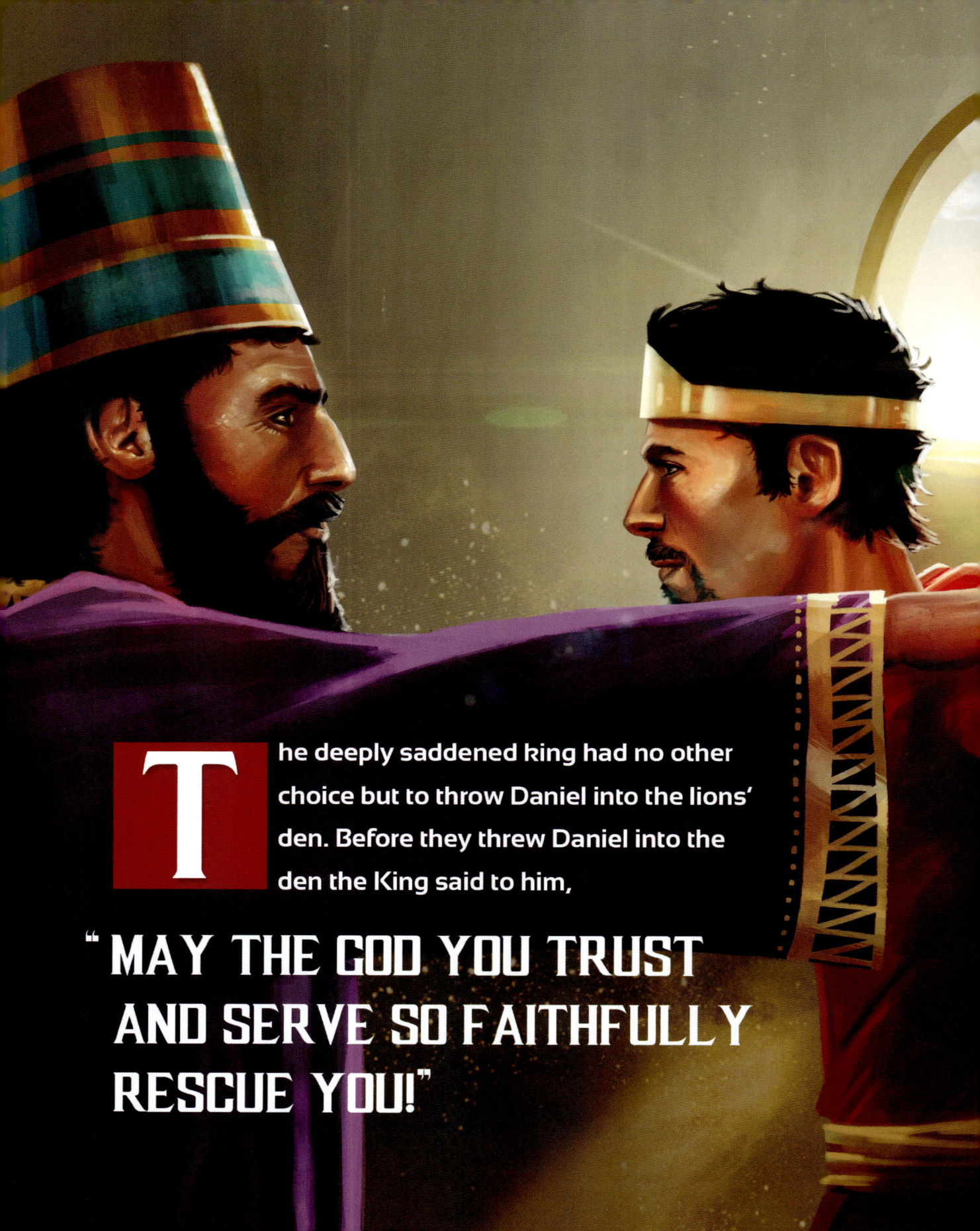

The deeply saddened king had no other choice but to throw Daniel into the lions' den. Before they threw Daniel into the den the King said to him,

"MAY THE GOD YOU TRUST AND SERVE SO FAITHFULLY RESCUE YOU!"

They threw Daniel into the den and placed a stone over the entrance to make sure he wouldn't escape.

AS THE STONE SEALED THE CAVE, DANIEL LOOKED AROUND TO SEE ALL THE LIONS AROUND HIM; HIS FAITH NEVER WAVERED.

The king returned back to his palace and spent the night fasting. He refused to let any palace musicians play their music as they usually did. He had no peace and was not able to sleep that night.

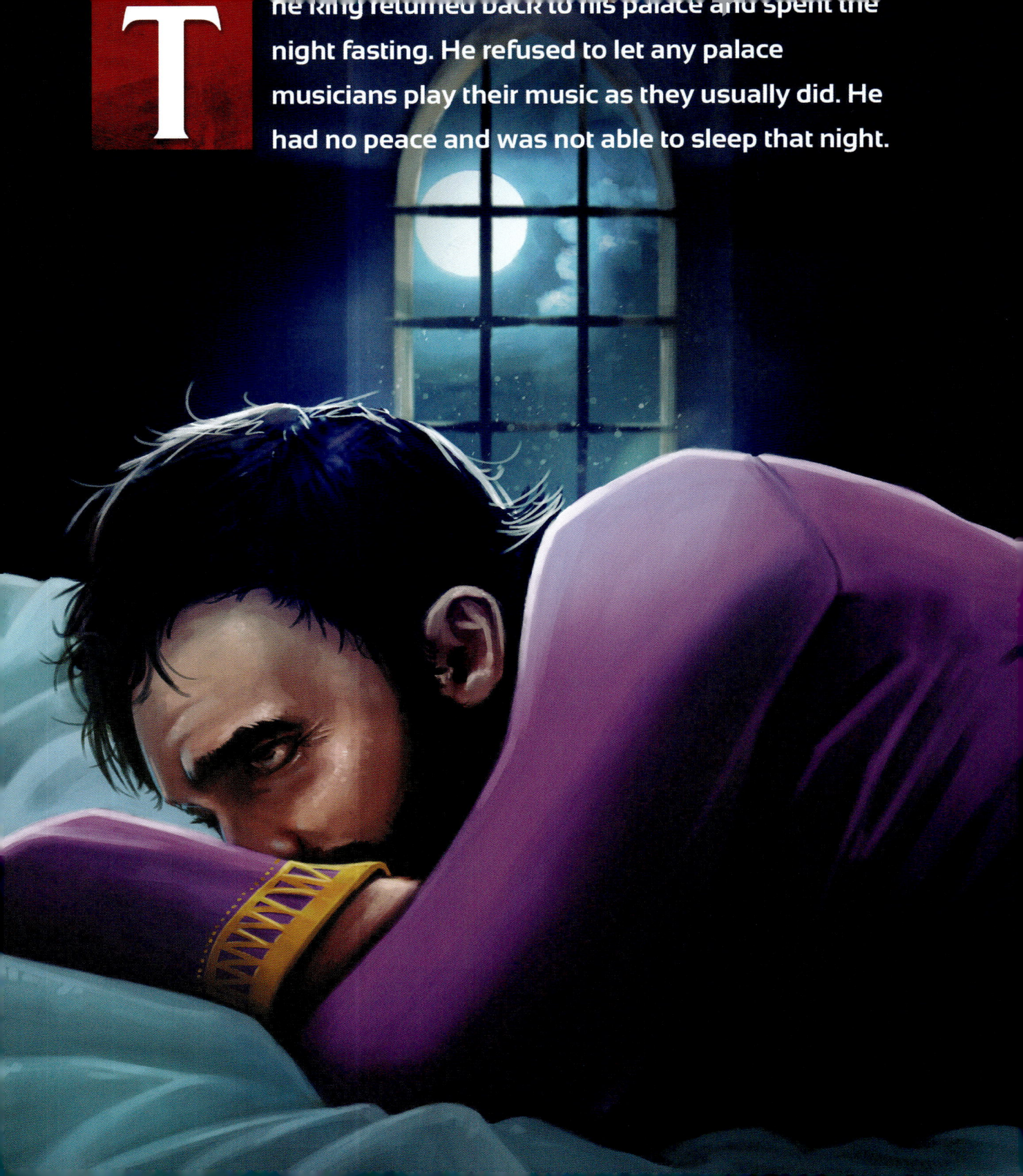

Very early the next morning, the king rushed out of the palace to get to the lions' den. When he got there he yelled out "Daniel, servant of the Living God, was your God able to rescue you from the fierce lions?"

Daniel answered, "Long live the king! My God sent his angel to shut the mouths of the lions so they couldn't hurt me. I was found innocent in God's sight, and I have done no wrong to you, Your Majesty."

The king was so happy to hear the good news.

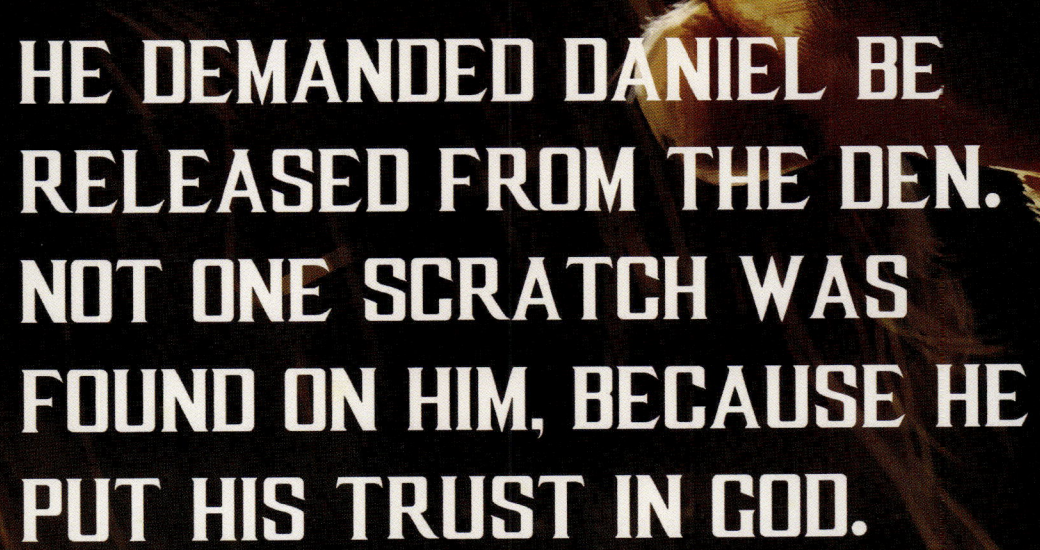

HE DEMANDED DANIEL BE RELEASED FROM THE DEN. NOT ONE SCRATCH WAS FOUND ON HIM, BECAUSE HE PUT HIS TRUST IN GOD.

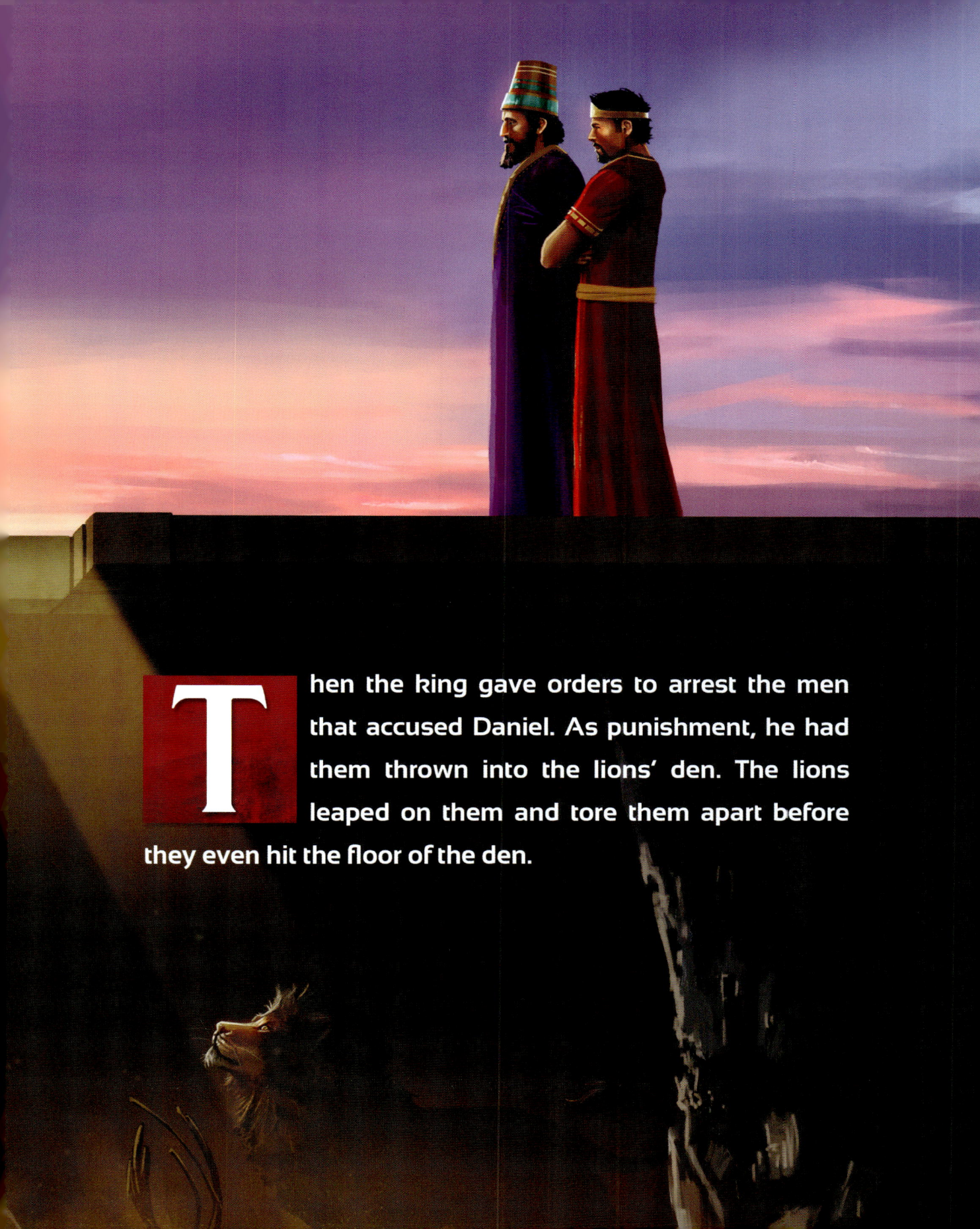

Then the king gave orders to arrest the men that accused Daniel. As punishment, he had them thrown into the lions' den. The lions leaped on them and tore them apart before they even hit the floor of the den.

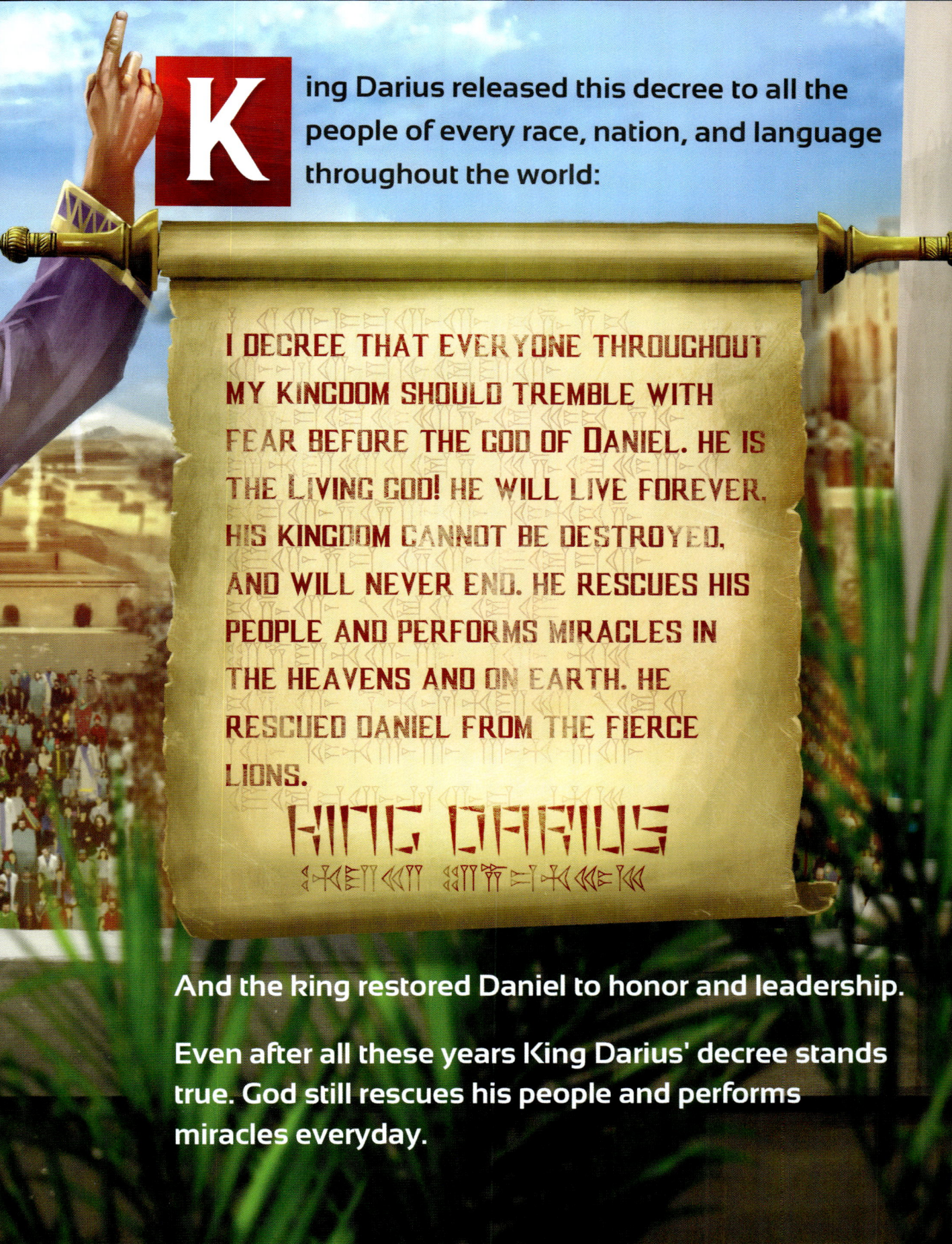

King Darius released this decree to all the people of every race, nation, and language throughout the world:

I DECREE THAT EVERYONE THROUGHOUT MY KINGDOM SHOULD TREMBLE WITH FEAR BEFORE THE GOD OF DANIEL. HE IS THE LIVING GOD! HE WILL LIVE FOREVER. HIS KINGDOM CANNOT BE DESTROYED, AND WILL NEVER END. HE RESCUES HIS PEOPLE AND PERFORMS MIRACLES IN THE HEAVENS AND ON EARTH. HE RESCUED DANIEL FROM THE FIERCE LIONS.

KING DARIUS

And the king restored Daniel to honor and leadership.

Even after all these years King Darius' decree stands true. God still rescues his people and performs miracles everyday.

ABC'S of Salvation

Have you ever asked Jesus into your heart? Jesus said in John 14:6- "I am the way. And I am the truth and the life. The only way to the Father is through me". If you want to live a life of love, joy and peace, you need Jesus! How do you accept Jesus into your heart? It's as easy as A-B-C!

A **ADMIT** that you need Jesus in your life. The Bible says in Romans 3:23, "All people have sinned and are not good enough for God's glory." Sin is the thing that blocks God from our lives. That's why God sent His Son, Jesus-- to forgive us of all the bad things we've done.

B **BELIEVE** that Jesus is God's son, sent to this earth to die on the cross for your sins, your healing and your success.

C **CONFESS** Jesus as your savior! The Bible says in Romans 10:9, that "If you declare with your mouth, "Jesus is Lord," and if you believe in your heart that God raised Jesus from death, then you will be saved."

It's So Simple!
Pray This after me.

Heavenly Father,

Forgive me of all my sins. Come into my heart wash me clean. Today, I make you my Savior, Lord and Friend. I am forgiven. I am a child of God. I am Mighty through Jesus Christ.

In Jesus' Name. Amen!

If you've prayed this prayer and accepted Jesus as your Lord, Savior and friend email us at:

info@themightyseries.com

and we will send you bible and a gift.

HooraaaY!!

ADALIS SHUTTLESWORTH
FOUNDER & AUTHOR OF THE MIGHTY SERIES